THE SACRED BOND

Preethi Srinivas
The Sacred Bond

Cover illustrations by Ajai Gautham

Published by BooxAi

ISBN: 978-965-578-061-1

THE SACRED BOND

PERSONAL EXPERIENCES OF COWS TOUCHING HUMAN LIVES

PREETHI SRINIVAS

CONTENTS

INTRODUCTION

I have been one of the many in this world to experience unconditional, non-judgemental love and acceptance from cows and bulls. Being immersed in a few cow shelters and sanctuaries has been one of the most gratifying and humbling experiences that has helped me deeply learn about people and their feelings towards cows. Through this experience I have learned three things: the first is that cows and bulls play a very important role in our ecosystem - their absence can significantly impact our well-being. Their compassionate and unconditional giving can never be remunerated. The second is that the definitions and belief systems on animal welfare and ethics vary from one part of the world to the other, sometimes pushing cattle towards danger. The third is that someone will miraculously emerge to create practices that not only save and protect cattle, but also help revive broken systems and build new thriving ecosystems.

The underlying principle is simple. Human beings are inherently related with cows and bulls: both care about each other and both can co-exist as friends and thrive in a mutual, symbiotic relationship - irrespective of the human being's background, religion, and belief system.

Human beings have historically co-existed in a mutual, loving relationship with cows and bulls. For instance, cows are an embodiment of divinity in the ancient Vedic civilization, while they are also personified as symbols of love, beauty and motherhood in the Egyptian civilization. Bulls, on the other hand, play a key role in farming and agriculture in several civilizations, including African, Roman, Greek, Indus Valley, and Chinese, to name a few. Consuming beef was historically a strict dietary restriction in most of the world.

The innate relationship between cows and human beings has been rocky in recent years. Industrialization has shifted the relationship to be more extractive and transactional, where cows and bulls are seen as commodities of milk, meat, and leather. Agriculture doesn't include bulls anymore, leaving them as a source of meat, leather, and several other products. Mindless consumer behavior has shifted dairy consumption, causing cows to act as milk supplying machines. There are several controversial climate debates on cattle's existence and a plethora of movements on plant-based diets across the world.

The falling-out in the sacred relationship between human beings, cows, and bulls continues to grow.

This book is meant to revive the lost relationship, to remind us that cows and bulls are our friends. This anthology is a celebration of the sacred bond - the serendipitous interactions resulting in the formation of a loving friendship between human beings and cows. For Nilesh, a friendship is established with Swathi, while for Nate and JP, it is with Raymond.

This book also compiles the consequential outcomes from the encounters, which led to the resuscitation of broken or the establishment of new, thriving ecosystems. For Kabilan, this is in the form of up-lifting the pastoral community in India; for William, this is in the form of guiding dairy farms to pursue cow-centered milking practices in Vietnam; while for GoPals, this is in the form of empowering the farming community in India.

Sometimes the sacred bond involves human beings going all out to protect the cows and bulls. For Soma, this is tracking down a Buddist from transporting cows for slaughter in Thailand; for Nuepane, this is climbing a hill or riding a motorbike to rescue stray calves in Nepal; for Amma, this is stopping a truck to buy cows that are en-route to a slaughterhouse in India; for Sankar, this is facing a racist violence in the US; and for Sai, this is negotiating with butchers in a cattle market in South India.

And sometimes, the cows and bulls act as saviors, helping heal human beings: for Lawrence, it is a transformative experience at his friend's farm in Australia; while for Sripriya it is spiritual healing from a dreadful past when she serves cows that visit her house in India.

In all these instances, in every story in this book, one would find acts of selfless service, resulting in unconditional love and respect between human beings and cattle.

* * *

In my first encounter with cattle, I stood facing a bull, over 7-foot tall, weighing over 1000 lbs, directly looking into my eyes. Nandi had a halter and a rope around him, but I knew he was capable of breaking loose if he chose to. But he stood still, welcoming me into his space. Being a small person in size and feeling, I chose not to walk away, because his calm demeanor drew me in.

Fast forward a few weeks, I became a frequent visitor, often visiting to offer service. This opportunity led to the formation of a lovable friendship with Nandi and several other cows and bulls at the shelter. Prior to my first encounter, I questioned my existence. Having had a lived experience of feeling broken, rejected and betrayed, I had built a strong wall around myself - Nandi broke down the wall.

A few months into volunteering, I found myself looking for *gaushalas* or cow sanctuaries to visit during my travels. Immersing myself in cow shelters and building friendships with cows and bulls transformed my life. The learnings from this experience inspired me to not only offer service, but also uplift stories and the efforts of people around the world who participate in a sacred relationship with cows and bulls. *The Sacred Bond* is a product of this inspiration.

I hope this book inspires you in this way too, for the truth is that cows and bulls exist globally and play a key role in our ecosystem. They are our friends. The sacred bond can be revived by giving unconditionally and receiving in gratitude.

CHAPTER ONE
A FATHER TURNED HERO

It is a late morning on a Sunday. Soma is sitting at his friend's coffee shop right outside a rice farm spread across 13 rai of land in Nong Bua Daeng, a district of Chaiyaphum province. He feels a burst of hot air brush his hair as he looks around casually at the shop he has been to several times. This time though, he is paying attention to the furniture, observing the table arrangements and chairs next to his own. Surrounded by a beautiful mountain range, the coffee shop is one of the well-known stopping points that serves fresh beverages and snacks for travelers to the nearby villages. The weather has been harsh this summer, making travel challenging for many. Consequently, there is not much traffic at the shop on this particular day.

Soma drifts away in thoughts about his second daughter who is safe at his home in Malaysia. His friend, Ubolthan, breaks the silence as she walks towards his table.

Sipping into her hot tea, Ubolthan inquires, "How's your daughter handling pregnancy?"

Soma is brought back to reality. Shaken, he responds, "Uh? Oh, yes, she is well... tough but handling it anyway." The iced tea offers much refuge from the heat and the long drive he had made from Bangkok to the shop. "How's the farm going?" asks Soma, to which Ubolthan responds, "There has not been much rain this season."

"Ah, it is very hot lah, but you are so far away from Bangkok city. It is really peaceful here." Casual exchanges inquiring about the well-being of family members continue as Soma notices an open lorry stop at the coffee shop. An old man wearing cotton trousers and a shirt with patches descends from the truck.

Ubolthan walks over to help the old man. "One cup of iced tea, please," says the old man as he adjusts his worn-out hat showing off gray hairs and wrinkles on the forehead. "30 Baht," Ubolthan says as she begins to prepare the tea. He places the money on the counter and looks away into the farm as he waits for his order.

Soma catches sight of some cows in the lorry. He sees a tall, sturdy white cow standing next to a young calf and another old cow sitting at the edge of the lorry. The old cow, seemingly worn out from the travel, moves herself by sticking her leg outside the truck.

Interrupted from his lost thoughts, the old man walks over to the truck to tether the leg of this cow with a rope to prevent her from falling as he drives. Ubolthan walks over to the truck and hands over the old man's order. They make a few exchanges, following which she walks back to sit with Soma.

"What's happening? Who is he and why does he have these cows?" asks Soma. "The cows are being taken to be slaughtered," responds Ubolthan. Soma is taken aback. Thoughts race in his mind as he thinks of his pregnant daughter. The concept of a mother cow and her calf being slaughtered sends shivers down his spine. Without a moment to waste, Soma inquires, "If I save the cows will you be willing to keep them in your farm?" Ubolthan smiles and, without hesitation, says, "Of course." Silence falls, Soma is relieved to have found a place to house the cows. He begins to mentally calculate how he would manage to pay for the cows. "I want to save the mother and her calf," he thinks to himself.

"It's a hot afternoon, how's everyone doing?" The silence is broken by Ubolthan's sister Yam. Ubolthan narrates Soma's decision, following which her sister, Yam, uncovers the backstory to where they can find the old man and the cows. "He is most likely going back to his village, which I think is the one that is a few miles away.

Normally these people will dock the cows there and take them out to the slaughterhouse in the evening. Let's go look for him," she says.

* * *

Soma looks outside the window to see rice fields as Ubolthan drives the car to the nearby village. He is apprehensive. Thoughts race through his mind as he imagines all possible outcomes that could or could not lead them to saving the cow and her calf.

He keeps bouncing from thoughts about his daughter to that of seeing a cow and a calf tethered to ropes in the truck. "We will be there shortly," comforts Ubolthan, understanding his anxiety as she places her hand over his.

As they enter a narrow village road, they see an old cow lying on the ground within the compound of a house next to a cow shed. On getting closer, they identify the truck they had been looking for. The old man walks outside from the shed. Soma walks over to the old cow, only to find that she is blind in one of her eyes. He sees the old man pull the cow to make her move. "Gosh, it seems like the cow has already given up on her life," Soma wonders.

Ubolthan and her sister approach the old man and suggest they would like to buy the mother and her calf. As they negotiate, three other cows from inside the shed start walking towards them. Ubolthan notices tears in their eyes. "The cows could be pregnant," Ubolthan declares.

Soma is moved to see the cows express their need for freedom from being slaughtered. "It looks like they are aware of their fate, they look very afraid," concurs Soma.

"I am surprised you want to buy the cow. People here eat beef, and raw beef is a delicacy," says the old man. "This is for a good cause," responds Ubolthon. She adds, "You are a Buddhist, we hope you understand." The old man looks at Soma and his friends closely. After a moment of thought, he changes his mind. He nods in agreement indicating his willingness to sell the cow and her calf.

Soma leaps at this opportunity and takes Ubolthan aside. "I originally wanted to buy the mother and her calf, but I see more cows here. I don't want to leave the old cow as well," he whispers. Ubolthan understands Soma's feelings and negotiates with the old man to buy all six cows. They agree, shake hands and the cows are saved!

Soma drives back to Bangkok as Ubolthan works with her sister to arrange for transportation to bring the saved cows to her cousin's farm for temporary housing. She works with her family members and employees to set up a cow shed in her farm, two weeks following which, the cows are brought to what eventually turns out to be a Cow Sanctuary. Two months into managing the cows, she is visited by a Monk, who, after coming to know about the Cow Sanctuary, brings four more cows he had saved from slaughter.

A congregation of devotees visit the farm and offer sacred prayers with the presence of Buddhist monks, which makes the place much more auspicious.

* * *

Four months pass. "She gave birth to a calf!" Ubolthan exclaims over the phone, as she wipes tears of joy rolling from her eyes. This is one of the saved pregnant cows that had given birth. Soma is beyond ecstatic as he responds, "I am coming there this weekend, lah, send me photos and videos." After the call, Soma flips through the photos. He notices the sacred white sign of a Bodhi Leaf on the calf's forehead.

"This is considered as an auspicious sign by Buddhists," he thinks to himself. He takes a deep breath and looks over the counter at his daughter sitting on the couch. He feels a sense of exuberance as he shares the happy news with his daughter and plans his weekend trip to the farm.

CHAPTER TWO
THE BOVINE BIKER

The rising sun casts a golden hue across the morning sky. Neupane passes a small group as he makes his way from Guhyeshwari Shaktipeeth to Kirateswar Mahadev temple in Kathmandu, Nepal. He nods and smiles at the group. "All well, Gopal dai?" asks a person from the group. Nuepane smiles and says, "Can't be better!" He hurries past the group so he can make it on time for the morning service. As he continues to walk energetically, his attention is drawn towards the Pasupatinath forest. He slows down and looks at his watch. "I have a few more minutes, why don't I walk through Mrigasthali?" he considers, "it is a beautiful day today," he concludes and decides to take the detour.

Neupane sights four deers running as he proceeds to walk into the beautiful forest. He grins. Ordinarily, he wouldn't have a chance of catching one but there were four of them, how could he miss? "This is so good," he reflects, he hadn't been on this route for several months. "Gosh, I feel like climbing the stairs," he says to himself.

Neupane looks up and around to see the spring sunlight beaming through the trees. He observes the rocky hill and the trees flanked on either side of a flight of stairs. He pulls his sleeves up and takes a step forward, watching, hoping to spot more deers as he ascends.

As he continues his hike, he hears a sound. He piques his ears, "What's that sound?" He continues to listen intently. "Wait, that sounds like a calf," he bursts. He looks around, scanning his surroundings to spot the source of the sound. Neupane spots a calf at the top right of the hill. He looks at the stairs that lay ahead of him and the calf that is calling for help. "How do I do this," he muses, "there is no path. I am going to have to climb the rocks." He places his right foot out the stairs onto the rocky hill. After a moment, he bends over to place both his hands, lifts himself and places his other foot onto the rocks so he is on all fours. "That was not bad," he thinks. He slowly shifts his body weight to move his limbs so he is able to move upward towards the calf.

A few minutes pass as he slowly makes his way up. As he reaches close to the calf, a rock falls beneath Neupane's feet. He manages to feel a ledge to get more support. His adrenaline surges, urging him to do what he would have otherwise considered not achievable. He does not have a rope or rails to hold onto, neither does he have a soft mat to land on. Neupane closes his eyes and takes a deep breath. Without further deliberation, he heaves himself up to join the calf in a small flat area.

To his surprise, Neupane finds himself facing two calves, one that is stuck in a pit, while the other that has called out to him for help.

* * *

Neupane is breathing hard. He pants as he attempts to lift the calf from the pit. "Hmm, he seems lightweight to me," he utters as he struggles. He looks around, scanning the environment as he continues to determine his plan of action for rescuing the calf. After a few attempts at tugging, he declares, "I need a break." He looks towards the stairs and sights the group of people he had passed on his way to the forest.

"We need help!" he yells. The group rushes up the stairs. One of the group members asks, "What are you doing there, Gopal dai?" to which Neupane responds, "A calf is stuck in an uncomfortable pit, we have to save him. Please, help." The group members look at each other, surprised. One of them responds, "Who would risk their life for an animal? Come down, it is dangerous!"

Neupane nods his head in disagreement. "What do I do now?" he ponders as he caresses the calves. The free calf moves closer to Neupane, lovingly receiving his massage. "Maybe I can ask for help at the Mrigasthali police station," he wonders. Moments pass as Neupane witnesses the calf's discomfort. He decides to give his only idea a try. Neupane slowly retraces his way down the rocks, to the stairs and rushes to the police station.

"We will send nine men," says the inspector. Neupane is beyond glad that he has managed to obtain assistance and that the calves will be saved soon. The group make their way back to the rocks and finally manage to rescue the calves. Recognizing that the calves may be hungry, Neupane proceeds to cut some grass from the forest and offer them to the calves.

Moments pass. The men who had stepped up to help Neupane leave to get back to their lives. Neupane had forgotten his visit to the temple. "I wish I could bring more food to these little ones," he fantasizes. After one final ritual of caressing, he bids goodbye to the calves and heads home.

* * *

Several months pass. Neupane has managed to set up a cow shelter. Housing over 160 bovines, this shelter cares for stray bulls and ill, non-productive cows. As a part of rescuing cows, Neupane travels on his motorbike every day to locate and bring back stray calves so they have a permanent home.

It is midday. Neupane works his way through feeding and spending time with the shelter animals. He is outside, surrounded by a few cows as he continues to offer them some fruits. "Gopal dai, don't forget to eat your meal today as well!" calls out a worker. Neupane looks around at the worker, grinning. "So many people stop by this shelter to eat free meals, but you don't get to eat," the worker exclaims. He adds, "Please, eat something before you step out to look for stray calves this afternoon."

Neupane nods, looks back at the cows, caresses them lovingly and walks into the building to eat his first meal for the day.

It is later that afternoon. Naupane gets onto his motorcycle, a 150cc commuter. He is accompanied by his helper. They head out on a quest to locate and rescue another calf. Neupane skillfully zigzags through the traffic as he navigates to find areas with trees. The pair attentively scan the environment during their journey. After a few miles, Neupane sights a calf behind a thick shrub. He stops the motorcycle and the pair get off to get closer to the calf, only to fear the calf off.

"Get on the other side," instructs Neupane. He runs behind the calf, but the calf is much faster than him. "Help!" Neupane calls out, "we need to catch this calf," he yells. A few passersby stop to assist with Neupane's operation. After a few moments of pursuit, the group manages to surround the calf. One of the members walks closer to finally get hold of the calf. Neupane and his helper return to the shelter that evening with an additional passenger, the rescued calf. The calf is cleaned and vaccinated.

Later that evening, Neupane decides to pay a visit to the calf. He sits next to the baby bull, slowly stroking him as he drifts away in his thoughts. "It is such a strange world," he thinks, "we consider cows as Lakshmi, our mother, yet people consume all the milk from her and let her go once she is no longer productive."

He continues, "People tie a piece of cloth around the eyes of the newborns and bulls and leave them in some difficult place so they cannot find their owners." He takes a deep breath and attempts to discern his feelings, "Stray cows are in danger of consuming plastic and dehydration. All of this is so painful." He continues to mull as tears well up his eyes, "If cows are our national animal, shouldn't the government do something for their welfare?"

Neupane's thoughts are interrupted. The calf nods and places his head on Nuepane's lap. Neupane smiles and fondles with the calf's ears. He looks into the calf's eyes and says, "I want to see a proper management system for cows before I die." He pauses for a moment and continues, "I will do anything to make that happen, I promise."

CHAPTER THREE
UNHOOKING FOR FREEDOM

"He is coming across as aggressive. Let's go."

"Paapa, we should not leave here without the cows…"

* * *

Nilesh's family had just returned to the US from India, where they had managed and cared for nearly 50 cows every day. Apart from a handful of new acquaintances, the family knew no one in Houston. But they function as a single unit that believes in protecting and loving cows. Being a part of the Goswami lineage, this family has a deep connection with cows.

A little over two years ago, Nilesh's father, Abhinav, a data-scientist by profession, had let go of a high-paying job to move the family back to a village in India to care for cows. Nilesh's mother, Pratibha, was in-tune with her husband's desires and ensured she pulled the family together as they navigated differences in the standards of living.

His elder sister, Kanu, had an equally strong personality for loving cows and partnered with him in sharing everyday chores. Little did they anticipate that they would return back to the US in an attempt to replicate their success from their hometown in India.

Back in the US, the Goswamis had just settled into a new home with an attached farm. With the kids attending classes at a local school, and Abhinav working remotely, things seemed pretty stable for the family to function. A few days into settling, the family decided to shop around for cows of Indian origin to bring home.

* * *

Nilesh is breathing hard, with tears rolling down his eyes. He looks back and forth between his parents and the cows at a local ranch in Texas. He wipes beads of sweat on his forehead as he reaches into one of his pockets. Sixteen-year-old high schooler, Nilesh, is an ardent lover of cows. The opportunity to take care of cows in his early teens laid the foundation for his strong opinions about cows and their role in the world. He understands cows and interestingly, cows understand him. They share a very special bond.

Nilesh sees seven cows staring at him, their eyes filled with fear. The cows at this ranch had lost hope in life as they awaited death. They see the farmer on this ranch as a representation of death, a human that controls their life.

Nilesh bursts out, "You are seeing the cows, it is not fair to them. And you heard the rancher, he doesn't know what he is doing. We can't let these cows suffer and eventually die."

"He's right, we should do something," adds Geetha, one of the new friends the Goswamis had made since their move to Texas.

"I understand, but we can't just act out of emotion. Let me negotiate…" says Abhinav.

* * *

The sun is about to go down in a few hours. Nilesh and Geetha had spent several hours overnight meticulously preparing the farm for the cows. A truck arrives at the entrance of Nilesh's house. He runs out overjoyed, for he had been anticipating the arrival of the cows that he had advocated to bring home just a day ago. He grins at the truck driver and opens the gate while slowly counting the number of cows he can spot from the window.

Nilesh runs over to meet his father at the truck. Excited, he calls for his mother and sister to come out and watch the cows enter their farm, their home. The family had invited a few other acquaintances to visit and had already picked out names for the cows. Everyone is awaiting the opportunity to call out the names with the expectation that the cows would come running towards them, their saviors.

A middle-aged American steps out. The red flannel shirt and blue jeans stand out against the green background painted by the lush grass on the farm.

He adjusts his baseball cap and looks around the farm. He starts to small-talk with Abhinav as Nilesh anxiously waits for the cows to be let out. "The sun is about to go down, why is this person delaying the process?" he wonders. The cows were finally let out after several minutes of conversation.

"They are here!" he exclaims, beaming with a bright smile. Little did he know that the next few moments would be a turning point in his life.

* * *

"Get a stick, let's try to round them up," shouts Pratibha.

"They are moving very fast," responds Geetha.

"We have lost four of them!" adds Nilesh.

People watch helplessly as cows run away from the farm. Nilesh stands in the middle of the farm, frozen, failing to comprehend the events from the last few minutes. His heart races as he scans the farm to see if he can spot the cows. "Maybe they are being playful," he thinks. "But that wouldn't make sense, why would they want to play now? Unless...the farmer had attempted using a painful approach while bringing the cows here," he ponders.

Nilesh watches as people around him scramble and run to look for the cows. He runs as well, but he is heartbroken. The cows had learnt to not trust humans anymore, even if one went out of the way to save them.

Nilesh is pained to observe how the fear of abuse and distrust in humans had motivated them to run.

The group searches the neighborhood all night only to return home unsuccessful. The search continues the following morning with the hope of bringing the cows home before Nilesh's classes begin. Success strikes at 5 in the morning when three cows are identified. But one, fondly named Swathi, is still left to be brought home.

The next few weeks are filled with pain as Nilesh watches his family struggle to get assistance. Friends visit to offer support and volunteer to assist with going out into the nearby woods, but it doesn't help improve the situation. Although distracted, he is hopeful. He prays, everyone in his family prays, everyone who believes in Goswami's mission prays, for they hope and wish for a supreme power to bring Swathi home.

* * *

"We identified a cow in the woods near the highway exit. We need help bringing her home. Can you help us, please?" Nilesh overhears his father speaking on the phone. "Who could that be?" he wonders. "I don't understand, what do you mean?" Nilesh continues to hear his father speak. "Let's do lasso."

Abhinav had just hung up the phone. Several neurons spark in Nilesh's brain as he tries to form a rational connection to what he had overheard. "I am sure paapa is asking someone for help. Lasso... I can think of cowboys. I wonder what's going to happen next!"

"The cowboys are coming tomorrow," announces Abhinav.

"What will they do?" inquires Nilesh.

"They suggested tranquilizer or lasso for bringing Swathi home. Both are going to hurt her, but the hope is lasso is not as life-threatening as tranquilizer. We will just have to hope for the best," responds Abhinav.

* * *

Nilesh has a tough time sleeping that night. The thought of Swathi getting hurt torments him. "It doesn't have to be this way," he thinks to himself as he uncomfortably rolls from one side to the other in his bed. "We should let her live the way she wants, it is alright if she doesn't want to come home… she can live in the woods… but what is the guarantee that someone will not harm her?" Nilesh battles his thoughts as he imagines multiple possible outcomes leading up to Swathi's death. After several failed attempts at calming himself down, he wakes up to get himself a cup of water. On his way to the kitchen, he sees Abhinav sitting on the couch in the living room. Abhinav looks concerned.

"Are you not sleeping?" asks Nilesh.

"Uh? Yes, I will… in a bit. What are you doing at this hour? Shouldn't you be asleep?" says Abhinav. Their dialogue is interrupted by Pratibha, "Are you guys not sleeping?" as she and Kanu walk out from the neighboring bedroom.

The family sat in the living room in silence. The night passes. The Goswamis do not sleep. No one speaks about Swathi or their concerns. Each person silently battles their anxiety for what lies ahead.

* * *

It has been two days since Swathi was brought home. Housed inside a barn and still in an enormous amount of pain, she is beginning to recognize her surroundings. Meanwhile, the Goswamis had fenced their farm, which prevented cows from running away. But that did not solve the cold war that was uprising.

Swathi was brought home bleeding, with a part of her ear cut by the lasso. Nilesh and his family had spent the past 48hrs tending to Swathi while also caring for the other cows. Seeing Swathi struggle in pain deeply impacted not only the Goswamis, but also the other cows. The fear of humans amplified in the cows. They ran to the other end of the farm every time a human approached them, even if they were being offered food. The Goswamis had expected to establish a rose garden where beautiful roses as cows thrived. But what had transpired from the recent incidents was a garden with a handful of buds and thorns.

Nilesh grapples with the situation as he attempts to get past the strong barrier Swathi has raised up against herself. He did not give up, he persistently went back to feeding and making a connection, only to be pushed back. He strongly believed that cows are compassionate, docile beings.

"They will definitely go back to trusting humans, Swathi will come around," he consoles himself. The Goswamis try multiple techniques to establish a bond with all the cows. Nilesh continues to spend most of his time outside the school with Swathi.

Weeks pass. Swathi begins to heal. As time passed, Nilesh observed that Swathi acknowledged his presence when he sat next to her. She did not revolt as long as he did not touch her. With time, she allowed Nilesh to touch her. The bud of his relationship with Swathi is beginning to blossom. "I should let her take her time, but I want to ensure I am doing what is agreeable for her... I really wish we could get the halter out, it must be really uncomfortable for her," he thinks to himself.

Nilesh works with his father to remove Swathi's halter. And that was it! Suddenly everything falls in place. The relationship completely blooms into a beautiful rose with this pivotal act. This is the true freedom the cows wanted – to be themselves and live their lives. Moments after the halter is removed, Swathi stares into Nilesh's eyes as he did of hers. He sees tears roll down from her eyes as he feels his cheek wet from his own tears. She nods her head as he comfortably puts an arm around her neck and starts to pet her. She closes her eyes and places her head on his lap.

CHAPTER FOUR

A HAVEN FOR NURTURING RELATIONSHIPS THAT GUIDE AND HEAL

It is midday. The blue sky is dotted with fluffy white clouds drifting lazily with the gentle breeze. The afternoon sun bathes the lush green pastures, shining through the trees while creating mysterious shadows. A 2000-pound Jersey steer, who would otherwise be mistaken for an alpha animal, works his way munching on the pasture with great enthusiasm. His muscles ripple as he moves. He swishes his tail to ward off the flies and lifts his head to chew the grass that he has managed to uproot from the ground. The occasional swishing of the tail, followed by the moving of the head up and down, results in an orchestrated act, much like a choreographed dance.

It has been a busy morning for Nate. He is standing a few feet away from the steer, lost in thought. A cool breeze blows as he zips up his jacket. He turns to look at the steer.

"Raymond looks golden-hued in this blazing sun," he thinks to himself. Contentment warms him from within as he continues to observe the steer, Raymond.

Nate drifts in his thoughts as he travels to his past, to a time when the week-old steer had arrived at the farm. His thoughts dance as he remembers the days when he bottle-fed Raymond. Happiness streaks through him like a comet as he visualizes Raymond as a young calf ripping the nipple off from the bottle as he gets closer to finishing its contents, only to have the remainder of the milk showered all over him. Nate chuckles and adjusts his cap. He stands engulfed in joy as he traverses his memories of Christmas eve every year since Raymond's arrival at the farm.

Nate jolts out from his trip through a delightful past, only to see Raymond standing right beside him. Raymond nudges Nate, encouraging him to massage him. In an almost telepathic communication, Nate understands Raymond and proceeds to stroke his neck. They are joined by an eight-year-old boy. JP, in his pair of jeans and red shirt, pants as he reaches them. With the eyes of pure mischief and a heart of gold, he moves with a spark and a smile that goes all the way through his core. "You are here," says Nate, to which JP inquires, "What are we doing today?" JP giggles and adds, pointing to Raymond, "Look at how he moves his tongue around his nose!" Nate responds with a smile, still continuing to stroke Raymond around his neck.

"We will go in to clean the stalls." Nate pauses and adds, "How's your day been?"

"It's been alright," responds JP.

"Can I touch him?" inquires JP, as he puts his arms around Raymond's neck.

"Easy there," says Nate. "Putting your arm around him may intimidate him," he adds and continues to probe. "Do you want to try what I am doing?"

JP shifts his weight from one leg to the other. He attempts to mimic Nate's bodily gestures as he moves his thin limbs, stroking Raymond's neck.

"There you go," says Nate as he continues to stroke Raymond around his ears. "He really likes it near his ears," Nate adds.

Nate steps back and watches as JP takes over and massages Raymond. Raymond closes his eyes and raises his neck, exposing portions of his body that he wanted being stroked by JP.

A few minutes pass. The air fills with engaging smells of urine and dung as Raymond begins to excrete waste. JP stops and looks up at Nate. "We should probably head back once he is done," says Nate. JP nods. Flanked on either side by Nate and JP, Raymond begins to walk back to his stall. Unthreatened by Raymond's huge appearance, JP walks alongside, holding Raymond's halter. A peaceful march across the property ensues with Raymond's majestic gait causing reverberating and earthshaking footsteps. JP chuckles and follows suit. He mimics Raymond's demeanor, holding his head high.

Once the party reaches the stall, Nate works with JP to situate Raymond. As Raymond sits down, Nate receives a phone call and steps out. In Nate's absence, JP decides to sit next to Raymond. He rests his head on Raymond's body and closes his eyes.

Silence falls as Raymond continues to hold JP, occasionally swishing his tail and moving his ears. They both ruminate, Raymond his cud, while JP his thoughts. "Your world is so calm," JP thinks. He continues to mull, "And fun." JP raises his head and sits up, opening his eyes. He stares into Raymond's eyes for a moment, then leans in and whispers into his ears, "You are the best, I love you!" Raymond moves to adjust his posture and proceeds to rest his head on JP's thighs. This cues JP to offer Raymond more massage around his neck.

"Alright, you can begin cleaning from the other end of the stalls," declares Nate. JP's brief stint of paling around Raymond is disrupted as Nate walks back into the stalls. JP gets up, straightens himself and proceeds to the first stall. "JP is very similar to the rescued animals in this farm," Nate ponders, "he needs to be adopted by loving people who can give him a forever home." He closes the door to Raymond's stall, and stays back to observe Raymond from outside his stall. Nate had just spoken with his wife and daughter on the phone. He draws his phone to see a picture of him with his wife and six-month-old daughter. Nate smiles and looks back at Raymond as he pockets his phone. He contemplates, "Watching you grow and gracefully change the lives of so many people around you is the most gratifying experience I will forever be grateful for." He leans in to stroke Raymond as Raymond lovingly reciprocates the gesture. Nate whispers, "Thanks to you, I am better prepared for fatherhood."

CHAPTER FIVE

SELFLESS AND COMPASSIONATE ACTS OF DHARMA

Sunlight peeps through a thick shade of trees and a cool draft of air places a sweet kiss on everyone's forehead as it proceeds to rustle the leaves. Four men standing under a large banyan tree take a moment to enjoy the breeze on an early Sunday morning as they negotiate the sale of a cow. People from around a small village had gathered that morning for the farmer's market, an event that occurs every few weekends, allowing farmers to sell their produce directly to their consumers from neighboring villages. Just like every other farmer's market, this one was crowded and noisy, with people calling out names of the produce and its prices. It was particularly a special morning that day, for it sowed the seed for the establishment of a cow shelter in a small, downtrodden village.

A thirteen-year-old bumps into one of the four men as they make their way towards the concluding remarks for their settlement. Gangadharan manages to stop himself from the sprint he had made impromptu in lieu of meeting the men before the cow is sold.

One of the men remarks, "Careful there, boy, why the rush?" to which he responds, "I will not let you sell her!" Silence strikes the farmers market as people stare at a five foot boy with ruffled hair, wearing a red colored-tank top and a pair of khaki shorts. A few whisper to their neighbor as Gangadharan raises his voice to speak with one of the men, "Father, all you need is money. Amma will give you the money."

Gangadharan pants as a million thoughts criss-cross his mind. "Amma has taught me to be nice to all living beings. I have seen Lakshmi grow up. How would I let her be taken away to be slaughtered?" He clenches his fist. "I am sure Amma will take care of this problem," he consoles himself. "But, will these men believe me? I have to act fast," he attempts to break himself free from his thoughts. "Amma is waiting to buy Lakshmi, she has the money, she will pay. Lakshmi is our family member, don't sell her to be killed, please," he pulls on the hand of his father. Gangadharan's father is flustered. He looks back at the other three men, helpless and guilt-stricken.

* * *

Gangadharan and his father make their way to Amma's house, a bungalow in a small neighboring village. Amma's ancestors had been associated with Swami Vivekananda and had played a vital role in the propagation of his message. Amma's acts of compassion towards all living beings, her selfless service, and her spiritual yearning are celebrated in the village.

In fact, Amma's illustrious acts of altruistic love have had a domino effect on the village members, with few households adopting and caring for stray animals. As they enter the driveway, Gangadharan and his father see Amma walk out of the front door. The natural sanctity of her offers an aura of positive energy, causing them to clasp their hands in salutation towards her as they see holiness in this fifty-year-old woman wearing an orange-colored saree and vermilion on her forehead.

Amma responds with clasped hands and smiles at Gangadharan. "He is attempting to sell Lakshmi," exclaims Gangadharan. Amma looks at Gangadharan's father and back at Gangadharan. "Amma, please pay him, all he wants is money. Let us take care of Lakshmi here," Gangadharan concludes. Undisturbed, Amma discusses with Gangadharan's father to understand why he was attempting to sell the cow. She comes to realize that taking care of cows is not affordable by many, often forcing them to a path of destruction, a path that could relieve humans from their social responsibilities, but at the expense of physically harming the cow. Amma's spiritual master had often advised her to spread the message about respecting and caring for motherhood. "Cows represent motherhood, this is an opportunity for me to show in action as opposed to preaching. One never gets into the bad path if they follow acts of morality, compassion, and truth," she thinks. Without a moment of hesitation, Amma decides to invite and care for Lakshmi in her house. And so begins her journey of selflessly caring for abandoned cows.

* * *

A few years pass. Amma watches out the window at lush, green vegetation as her car drives past farms. As she takes a deep breath to smell the fresh air, she notices a truck overtake her vehicle. The truck is open from behind, exposing a view of cows. This bizarre sight triggers Amma to know more. "Drive fast and stop the truck," she tells her driver. The car speeds to overtake the truck and stops right in front, preventing the truck from proceeding. "Can you please find out from the truck driver where he is going?" Amma instructs her driver to initiate a conversation with the truck driver.

"I am in a rush, why should I tell you?" revolts the truck driver. Intending to avoid a fight, Amma gets out of the car and walks over to the truck. She looks inside to find several cows, some really unwell and others normal, stacked with no space for them to sit or stand. She walks over to the truck driver and inquires, "Where are you taking the cows?"

"I am taking them to a different farm, I am in a rush. Why are you stopping me?" pushes back the truck driver, to which Amma responds, "Don't worry, just tell me the truth. It doesn't seem like they are being taken to a farm. I can pay the money if that is what you want." The truck driver is taken aback. He thinks for a moment and continues to deny, "No, no. Someone has already paid for them to be brought to their farm. I have to leave now."

Amma nods her head in disagreement, still lost in thoughts as she mentally determines her next step.

"I should not provoke him," she thinks to herself. "What do I do? How am I going to protect these cows?" she wonders as her heart races. As she continues to stall the truck driver, a police constable stops. The peculiar sight of a car stopped right in front of a truck, an old lady arguing with a truck driver in the middle of a road motivates the constable to investigate further.

"What is going on here?" questions the constable, to which Amma uncovers her inquiry, suggesting the constable to probe more. Several minutes pass as Amma's heart rate begins to normalize. "These cows have to be saved, if only this truck driver admits that he is on his way to the slaughterhouse," she thinks to herself. True to her belief, the truck driver ends up admitting his destination. Amma's ears perk up at the mention of the slaughterhouse, her heart begins to race. She jumps into the conversation and intercepts, "I can pay for the cows, I am already taking care of some." The constable and truck driver stare at her. "Are you sure? We need to investigate your place before we can help negotiate this sale," says the constable.

A few hours later, the cows land at Amma's house. "That's the last cow," says the truck driver. He looks at the cows, then at Amma. "You are indeed very unique," he remarks as he gets into his truck to head home. Amma turns to look at all the cows. She is excited to welcome the newcomers, she rushes and begins offering feed as she talks to them.

She thinks to herself as she brushes her hand over some of the cows' heads, "This story would have been completely different if the constable hadn't stopped by. Acting on compassion, selflessness, and dharma will indeed protect people... and the cows."

CHAPTER SIX

SOCIAL ACTIVISM BREAKS THE INTERLUDE FROM PASTORALISM

A middle-aged man walks out of his room as other members of the house hustle and bustle, preparing for the day. A piping hot coffee sits at the table. Kabilan picks up the cup as he manages to flip through messages on his phone. He skims through forwarded messages, mentally making a note to review them later in the day as he continues to stare into his phone. He pauses to take a sip of coffee before proceeding to check emails. A smile emerges from his face as he carefully reads the most recent unread email in his inbox. "Prepare for a 1-week service at Thirumohoor village," he reads aloud. He continues to read the rest of the email in silence as his smile widens. He has been designated as the coordinator for the university college National Service Scheme cadets to participate in a social service program the following week. The news pairs well with the energy boost from his morning coffee as he prepares to share his excitement with his students. He hurries to get to the university college.

Drops of water splash onto passersby from a large water fountain positioned in a rotunda at the university college campus entrance. Kabilan walks by with a spring in his step as a few drops of water wet his white shirt. Wiping, he makes his way to his first class for the day at Madurai Kamaraj University College. "This is going to be fun," he thinks to himself. Being a part of the Air Force Academy in India, Kabilan's father is a key role model for Kabilan to emulate in offering service for the community. Kabilan's father and his grandfather had carefully crafted Kabilan's personal life and career to be centered around a city, where he had privileged access to good shelter, food, healthcare, and education. To a greater extent, he grew up protected from his ancestral history, with very little knowledge about his lineage. "Class, we visit Thirumohoor next week for a week-long service. Let us gather more information on what needs to be done and get an action plan together," Kabilan announces.

* * *

The sun has set. Kabilan and his students had successfully set up tents for their weeklong stay at Thirumohoor. He steps out of his tent and sits next to a small group of students looking curiously at a far distance. Kabilan follows their line of sight. "Who are these people?" he asks as they curiously look at a small group of men with a large herd of cows. "We don't know, sir, should we talk to them?" asks one of his students. "Let's go," responds Kabilan. They walk over to the men and the cows.

"We are pastoralists," says one of the men from the group. "There are nearly a hundred cows here! What will you do with them?" questions Kabilan. The conversation continues as Kabilan and his students are educated about pastoralism in India. Intrigued by the conversation, Kabilan and his students continue to converse with the group of men every evening of their stay at Thirumohoor. Continued discussion with the group makes it evident to Kabilan about his lineage. On deliberating and connecting the dots from earlier conversations with his father, Kabilan concludes that his ancestors had practiced pastoralism, but had moved away from their tradition owing to challenges. "I see why my immediate family moved away from pastoralism, it is extremely difficult in today's world," he reflects. "What can I do to help this community?" he contemplates.

"Can we make a documentary film about them?" asks Kabilan to his students. "That is a great idea! I can help with making the video," responds one of his students. Discussion continues as a small group of volunteers step forward to participate.

Weeks pass. Kabilan's small volunteer team had successfully launched a documentary film about pastoralists in Tamil Nadu. The movie describes the lifestyle, challenges, and benefits of raising country cattle. Kabilan is optimistic as he proceeds to write books on the topic to spread awareness further.

The more time he spends deliberating on how he can help, the more he pushes forward with different ways of offering support. He brings together a group of 20 young, passionate individuals to form the Thozhuvam Trust. Under his guidance, this organization pushes forward with several research efforts to help establish evidence-based support for the benefits offered by indigenous cattle.

Irrespective of his persistent efforts, Kabilan begins to realize a lack of economic improvement in the pastoral community. He sees people struggling with basic expenses as they make ends meet. He observes cows suffering, with no access to grazing land and clean water. "Pastoralists are on the verge of giving up their traditional system of caring for country cattle. Everyone seems to acknowledge the problem, but no one wants to act," he worries.

Disappointed with his expectations not being met, he continues to speak about the topic to several people, "indigenous, country cattle are our identity. They are healthy and offer so many benefits to human civilization such as support for organic farming, generating sustainable energy, improving biodiversity, reducing forest fires, reducing carbon footprint...the benefits are numerous." Upset at his helplessness, he continues to spin in his efforts.

* * *

Months pass. "We should form a team of people who can bring the community and cattle together," says an official from NABARD-MABIF at the Madurai Agricultural College.

Several months of strenuous attempts finally pay off. Kabilan is sitting at a table with officers from NABARD-MABIF as they come up with a strategic plan for offering a safety net support for pastoralists. Kabilan is beyond excited for what lies ahead as he muses, "The interlude to city life is indeed good. I have more access being on the other side. I respect and acknowledge my ancestors much more and will strive to make a contribution to this community. Onto making the world better!"

CHAPTER SEVEN

COWS BECOME THE SAVIOR

It is Fall, the sun is about to go down. The door creaks as a middle-aged man, Lawrence, opens the gate to a farm in Goldsborough, half an hour south of Cairns, Queensland. He removes his sunglasses, exposing wrinkles around his eyes as he scans the farm to familiarize himself. Isolation from the pandemic lockdown and long work hours had deeply impacted his well-being, causing him to feel overwhelmed and depressed. The bright light from the sun causes a burn in his eyes. Lawrence puts his glasses back on and proceeds towards a house at the other end of the farm. He tugs at his backpack as his footsteps adjust to the change in landscape from gravel road to lush, green grass. Fresh air blows, causing his baseball cap to shift. As Lawrence adjusts his cap, he spots a few cows sitting in the middle of the farm. "Interesting…" he murmurs to himself as he welcomes the change to endless hours of virtual meetings that had left him feeling burnt out. He walks past the cows into the house, drops his bag and walks outside to meet his new acquaintants, the cows.

Lawrence is visiting his friend's farm that houses six hand-raised cows. He has had prior experience interacting with racehorses, which he had often thought were aggressive. "Not sure how this is going to work out, but they look very calm," he thinks to himself. "Hi there," he holds his hand out to a cow with a white-gray coat. She looks at him, not moving her posture, chewing her cud. He looks into her eyes, only to feel a sense of homecoming. A few tears roll down his eyes as he battles the plethora of feelings from his inner world. The strong barrier he had raised to protect himself from the outer world gives way. "Right," he says to himself, wiping the tears. He adjusts his gaze away from the cow to quickly glance at the other cows and is interrupted by his friend. "Great, you have met them," says his friend. Lawrence turns to face his friend who begins to walk towards the social gathering.

* * *

Weeks pass. Lawrence has settled into a routine of finding times on the day he chooses to work. It is midday Wednesday. He stares into his laptop screen, deep in thoughts, with one hand holding a cup of tea that has turned cold from being out for a long time. The sunlight gleams through the window, causing the entire room to be bright and well-lit. He is interrupted by a knock on the window. He looks out to find a cow staring at him. He looks back and forth between the cow and his laptop screen and sips the tea. "Eww, this is not good anymore," he says to himself.

He looks back at the cow and, after a moment of deliberation, closes his laptop and steps out to meet the cow.

Lawrence has gotten comfortable interacting with the cows as much as the cows have with him. He has memorized their names and has learnt to offer them gentle rubs in return to enhance his relationship with them. "Holly, here… let's walk over to the paddock," he gestures to the cow. They walk over to join the other cows. Lawrence spots the cow with white-gray coat. Her name is Milkshake. Milkshake has eaten well for the day and is about to rest. Lawrence had been avoiding close encounters with Milkshake since his prior intense and emotional experience with her. This particular day though, he picks up courage and walks over to her. He looks at her as she gazes into his eyes. He slowly sits down next to her as he begins to offer her gentle rubs. Within a few minutes, he is lying right next to her. Calmness settles as the barrier in his inner world crumbles. They both close their eyes and remain in silence for several minutes.

Lawrence's experience with the cows continues as weeks progress. He begins to recognize each cow has an individual personality, so much so that he feels like he has a new bunch of friends, each offering unique support for him to revive himself. Little did he know that this beautiful relationship was under threat.

* * *

"I will buy all of them," declares Lawrence.

He has been under the impression that the cows at his friend's farm were pets. His illusion is brought to a halt as he learns one day that the cows will soon be sold to a neighboring beef farm. "It is only a matter of time, they will soon be killed," he thinks to himself. "I should be able to pay for all of them using my savings," he concludes. "There is no way I am going to let the cows be killed… they are my friends," he validates his decision.

The following days seem very hazy to Lawrence as he navigates the world of managing cows. He had purchased the cows before thinking about how he would pay to take care of them. Stuck in a rut, he begins to wonder, "Cows have a therapeutic effect. They offered me comfort when I needed it the most." He continues to reflect on his experience, "I might not have a farm or the money to care for them, but I am convinced that others will also benefit from the calming effect that I experienced." A light bulb lights up in his mind as he continues to mull over his thoughts, "What if… what if I created a social enterprise that offered a paid service for assisting with promoting calmness and improvements to mental health in people?" He gets excited and rushes to his work desk, reaches for a scratch pad and jots down his ideas as he continues to brainstorm. "I should really set this up to assist with employing people living with mental illness, people with intellectual disabilities, and those who are neurodiverse," he continues. "Oh… and maybe, if I can make things work… I would love for this enterprise to educate the local community about mental illness and also offer a small portion of the profits for social good."

Lawrence steps back and looks at the notes he had scribbled into his scratchpad. Each letter shines like a beautiful engraving that had been sculpted. He smiles as he thinks to himself, "It would be more appropriate to state that these cows saved my life in comparison to me claiming I rescued them from being killed!"

CHAPTER EIGHT

A VIOLENT ACT LEADS TO MORE LOVE AND COMPASSION

"Hello, 911."

"Hello, this is Sankar. I am calling about a severed cow's head at my doorstep..."

"A what?"

"I am calling from Upper Mount Bethel Township. There is a severed cow's head at my doorstep. Can you please send someone to help?"

* * *

Sankar Sastri runs out to check on the animals on his 42-acre farm. "Sita... Nandu..." he continues yelling until he sees all the 20 cows emerge from the other end of the farm. His friend, Edye Huang, a former microbiologist and a volunteer at the farm, runs over to meet him at the fence. Sankar explains what he had sighted at his front doorstep. Huang, a strong believer in animal welfare, is equally shocked. She helps round up the animals to ensure everyone is safe.

Convinced all the animals on his farm were safe, Sankar walks back into the house from the backdoor. Having witnessed a severed cow's head at his front doorstep had completely shaken him, making him feel giddy. Trembling, he fills himself a cup of water and sits at the kitchen counter.

Sankar is wearing a pair of blue jeans and a polo shirt. He removes his Yankees baseball cap to wipe beads of sweat from his forehead and puts it back on. In an attempt to calm himself, he closes his eyes, only to see a flashback of events leading to where he is that Sunday morning. Moving to New York from India in 1964, he advanced in his career, eventually becoming a professor and the Dean of engineering at the New York City College of Technology. Flashing forward, his thoughts drift to the time post his retirement, when a Buddhist monk brought two cows for him to care for. He is reminded of the joy of seeing the farm grow and his move to the new farm just a month ago. He visually paints the cows' beautiful eyes in his mind, where he has often seen the reflection of divinity in the form of love and compassion. He pictures bonding and feeding one of the cows. "Sita, here, eat this." His thoughts drift to the times when he walks over to the fence, with the cows running out and romping around him like children. His musings are interrupted by the sound of a knock on his door.

* * *

"My name is Carrie, I am here to help. Do you know who did this?" a State Trooper had arrived on the scene.

"No, I don't know who did this and what they want. Maybe it's a prank. Or maybe something else is behind it," responds Sankar.

"I am going to ask you some more questions to help with the investigation..." says Carrie.

* * *

Sankar shifts in his bed as he struggles to fall asleep. Thoughts race through his mind. He is reminded of a scene from the movie *The Godfather*. "Could this be a warning? Well, it is a cow's head in the place of a horse. They didn't leave it on my bed, thankfully." With a plethora of thoughts pushing and pulling him in several directions, he tears as he leans into his faith. "While human mothers give their children milk for a few months, cows, our divine mothers provide milk for a lifetime," he ponders. He questions, "Why would anyone want to hurt the most loving and compassionate beings on Earth, when they should be treating them with respect?"

The night passes with brief moments of irregular sleep accompanied by introspective moments fueled by anxiousness. All he wanted post-retirement was to pursue a hobby of caring for and respecting cows.

He had managed most of the expenses financially out of his pocket, while there have certainly been times with donations flowing in to support his effort. Little did he know that he would make headlines over a tragic incident. "I really hope this is a prank and is not blown out of proportion," he thinks to himself. As he continues to mull over his thoughts, Sankar is overcome by a sense of compassion towards the person responsible for the incident. "Whoever did this is probably unaware of Sanatana Dharma and its principles. I can use this as a stepping stone to educate the local people about the principles," he declares.

* * *

Two months pass. Sankar has made peace with his thoughts and moved on to living in the moment, while still being prepared to face similar future events. In an attempt to express protest and to intimidate Sankar from an ethnicity perspective, a couple had left a severed cow's head at his front doorstep. Experiencing guilt, the couple turned themselves in to state police and confessed to the crime of buying and transporting a yearling cow's head at Sankar's front doorstep. While they were charged with multiple violations, Sankar put everything behind and pushed forward. Being a pragmatic person, he continued to pursue public education on topics related to protecting cows and choosing a vegetarian diet.

CHAPTER NINE

HEALING FROM A
DREADFUL PAST

It is a beautiful Spring morning. Two women sweep a street as a man drives past them to deliver newspapers to his customers. They nod and smile at each other. The trees carefully planted on either side of the street transform into a beautiful painting with a golden backdrop as the sun peeks out. A playful orchestration ensues with the man ringing the bell on his bike, the women moving their arms back and forth with their bangles, the roosters crowing, and the birds chirping. Dust rises and falls in an impromptu, choreographed dance, which transitions into a delightful performance as cows enter the street, adding to the ongoing orchestration, sounds from the bells around their neck. This spontaneous concert progresses to include only the sound of cowbells and eventually ends with the cows mooing as the cows walk past the women to a house at the end of the street.

"Ah, you are all here," says Sripriya jubilantly as she opens the gate to let the cows into her driveway.

"Surbhi, did you sleep well last night? Tulsi, how's your stomach? You didn't eat well yesterday…" Sripriya pauses to examine all the cows. As she carefully looks from one to the other, she inquires, "Is your owner taking good care of you all?" She smiles and pauses with hands on her hips for a response, to which a few cows respond by cleaning their mouth and nose with their tongue. A few others make friendly, playful noises and get closer to Sripriya, looking for a nice massage, while a few other naughty cows respond by urinating and defecating as they prepare for their first meal of the day. "Alright, alright. I know you are all hungry. Let us get you some food."

The cows move around to position themselves at their regular spots in the driveway, ready to eat as Sripriya scurries around to fill their buckets. She had taken extra care to prepare their meal overnight and ensured their buckets were clean for use. Bells jingle as supporting music to her voice as she begins to sing one of her favorite songs while placing a bucket filled with food in front of each cow. As the song comes to a close, Sripriya places the last bucket and declares, "…and finally, this one's for you, Ganga."

"Now, to get this place cleaned up while you girls finish eating," she continues. Sripriya walks over to get a broom and begins cleaning the driveway. The sound of bells jingling and those of the cows eating act as meditative music as she continues to sweep. She drifts into random thoughts that eventually take her back in time.

Visuals of a burning cow shed flash before her. She feels transported to an incident where she hears voices of cows crying out in pain and people crying out loud.

"Fire! Fire!"

"Quick, get some water!"

She sees some standing, watching the scene aghast, while some crying helplessly, beating their heads with their hands.

"Oh my God! Someone, please save them!"

Sripriya shakes in fear as tears roll down her eyes. She tries to shake herself out of this memory as she walks over to fill water into a large bucket for the cows to drink from. The temperature in the driveway drops as Sripriya crawls back into feeling sad. She continues to fill the water, struggling to forget an incident that had deeply impacted her. An incident that laid the foundation for developing a strong friendship between her and the cows. She stares into the bucket at her own reflection, questioning why cows from the incident were killed in a fire accident. "We were helpless," she thinks. "Where did we go wrong?" she questions, not noticing the water overflowing from the bucket.

A cow nudges her from the back. Startled, Sripriya looks around to find Tulsi looking at her mischievously. Sripriya is automatically transitioned back to today. She stops the water and looks over at Tulsi's empty bucket. "Ah, so you ate all the food today." She smiles and affectionately pets Tulsi as Tulsi looks deep into her eyes.

Sripriya follows, looking into Tulsi's eyes to find tears of love and compassion. She tears, her heart melts as the pain from the horrifying past chips away. A few more cows walk over to Sripriya to be petted. Sripriya begins to pet and massage the cows as they close their eyes in relaxation. Sripriya feels relaxed herself.

A silent conversation ensues between her and one of the cows, Surbhi. Surbhi listens without judging as Sripriya reflects, "I don't know why things happened the way they did that day, there must be a reason. We were all participating in service with good intentions." She pauses as she transitions over to massaging a different cow, Ganga. She continues to contemplate, "I don't know why I am feeding you all today, but I am very grateful for this opportunity. Your owner is milking you for money but is not feeding you well." Ganga continues to listen as Sripriya adds, "I love seeing you all every morning, I love being able to serve you, this is the best thing that can happen to me and I don't want to question how or why this is happening." Ganga opens her eyes to look at Sripriya with tears of gratitude. Sripriya tears herself and continues, "I am probably not going to forget the incident, but you are all helping me heal and move on from a dreadful past, thank you."

CHAPTER TEN

GOOD FOR THE COW IS GOOD FOR THE FARMER

The alarm sounds. There is tension in the air. A few men shout and scramble around as they decipher the cause of the alarm. William rushes towards the cows' resting place to meet a group of men. "Not again!" exclaims the manager of the dairy farm as the group looks at cows sitting in a pool of milk. "Move the cows and clean the area," instructs the manager to his workers. The day had not begun well for the people working at a dairy farm in North Vietnam that morning.

The manager joins William after having instructed his workers to continue the inspection of the farm. "This is not the first time this has happened," worries the manager. "We have tried everything to resolve this, but I think the issue is with the teats. As a consultant, what do you think we can do?" inquires the manager. William ponders for a minute. He pulls the sleeve on his white shirt and adjusts his baseball cap as he responds, "Let us go and inspect the cows."

"I really wouldn't think the problem is with the teats. My guess would be that they are not correctly milking the cows," William deliberates. He walks around, gently brushing the cows to ascertain his hypothesis. A few minutes pass, William continues to muse, "It is very important to follow a cow's cycle. She has to release the milk, anything forced is against nature and is not good for her." He turns around to face the manager and says, "Let us watch how you milk the cows later today."

William watches as a laborer checks the first milk, one cow at a time. The laborer meticulously moves between cows as he checks from one cow to another before coming back to cleaning every cow and finally attaching the machine for milking. William turns to the manager and says, "Your process for milking is incorrect." The bewildered manager stares at William, he looks back and forth between the milking station and William. "But... what could be wrong here?" he inquired. "You see, the hypothalamus of the cow is the center that generates a hormone called oxytocin," responds William as the manager perks up his ear to listen carefully. "This hormone helps the cow lactate. When you touch a cow, you are stimulating lactation. I see your men following an order for stimulating, cleaning, and then attaching the machine," adds William.

The manager nods in approval as William continues, "You spend a lot of time if you do this one task at a time for all the cows. The cows can get confused when you stimulate them, walk away and come back to clean, and then again to attach the machine. You really want to spend 10 to 15 seconds of uninterrupted stimulation and milking." William recognizes the confusion on the manager's face. He continues, "You can combine all the tasks for one cow at a time. This is much more efficient, hygienic, and less painful for the cow. Incomplete milking can lead to infection." The conversation continues as William advises and offers changes the farm could incorporate for the overall well-being of the cow. "Cow is the center of the universe. She needs room to walk around, fresh air, shade, lots of sleep and bonding with her calves. You need to keep the cows comfortable if you want good milk," he continues. The manager nods in approval as William resumes his proposed modifications. "The golden rule is to aim for longevity of the animal and avoid forced pregnancy. Even if she produces less milk, feed and love her. I will share some easy ways that have worked in the past in industrial setup like what you have here," he concludes.

"This has been really eye-opening," declares the manager as he walks William out of the dairy farm. "Thank you so much for taking the time to help us. We will be sure to incorporate your suggestions," adds the manager. "Glad I was of help," responds William as he gets into his car.

He smiles as he looks at the manager disappearing into the dairy farm from his rearview mirror and muses, "Good for the cow is good for the farmer."

CHAPTER ELEVEN

COW WASTE IS NOT TRULY A WASTE PRODUCT

Summer is about to wrap up. It is a fine afternoon. Cows rest peacefully in the sheds at the Ragavendra Gaushala near Malur, a town in Karnataka. The GoPals team sit outside the shed, under the shade of a tree, as they listen in silence to the snores from the cows. It has been a busy morning for the team. They had just wrapped up hosting a tour of the gaushala. The GoPals team have been bringing in urban families to multiple gaushala sites across the country to not only share information on the different breeds of Indian cows, but also offer a hands-on experience by creating a playful and engaging learning environment.

A cool breeze blows, causing the bells hanging around the cow's necks to move. A melodious jingle results as the team members continue to relish the moment of tranquility. The cows stop snoring. Some open their eyes to look around, while others adjust their posture as they proceed to continue their slumber. Silence falls.

"We should help the small-scale industry that this gaushala is attempting to create with cow-based products," says one of the team members. Others jolt out of their quietude. He continues as he looks around the facility, "We should plant medicinal herbs and other plants." "But there is not much water here and the topology is pretty mixed," muses another team member. Stillness falls as the team continues to ponder in silence. "This is actually good timing," says one other team member. "If we are done planting the saplings by the first week of June, we would have set up the system for six months of rain," he adds. "This is a great idea," says another team member. "We need to be thoughtful about how we are planting," she adds. Everyone nods.

* * *

Weeks pass. The multi-phase effort for holistically planting saplings around the gaushala at Malur has picked up momentum. Custard apple seedlings appear meticulously lined in the hillock area while those of tall, thorny plants take shape around the border of the facility. A large number of visitors have just been briefed about their day's activity involving planting seedlings of several flowering plants in the walk paths within the facility. Work begins in full enthusiasm.

"Eww, this smells bad," bursts out Mithun, a seven-year-old boy. He plugs his nose as he steps back from the cow, Lakshmi. It is Mithun's first time visiting a gaushala and experiencing the touch and smell of a cow at close quarters. "She is so big," he says.

Lakshmi looks into Mithun's eyes as she continues to stay calm and chew her cud. The calmness of Lakshmi lures Mithun. He steps forward towards her, looking into her eyes. Lakshmi lowers her head, allowing Mithun to touch her. Mithun strokes Lakshmi. His smile quickly turns into a curious elation as he watches a baby calf hop over to Lakshmi. Mithun giggles in delight as he watches the calf spring with her tail raised.

He turns around to meet a group of other children attempting to plant seedlings. "What is this?" he inquires. "This is Jeevamrutham," says one of the GoPal coordinators. Mithun watches in surprise as the coordinator puts her gloved hand in the mixture. "This mixture has been prepared from cow dung, urine, jaggery, pulse flour and some soil," she adds as she looks into Mithun's eyes. "Cow dung and urine are elixirs to protect our environment," she pauses to give Mithun time to digest the information thrown at him. After a moment, she continues, "They are filled with the nutrients that can bring life to the soil. In fact, they can also help support medical treatment for us humans." Mithun looks confused. He looks away, attempting to locate his parents and turns back to look at the GoPal coordinator. Understanding his confusion and distraction, the coordinator encourages, "It is alright, you can wear these gloves."

Mithun puts on a pair of gloves as he continues to listen with the rest of the group. "When you add this mixture, it will help the plant grow well," the coordinator continues to describe to the group of children. "Do you want this seedling to grow well?" she inquires as she looks from one child to the other.

Mithun shifts his weight from one leg to the other as he ponders. After a moment of consideration, he nods. "Then let us give this a try. Here, apply this mixture the way I am showing," adds the GoPal coordinator. Mithun nods and looks at a neighboring boy doing the same. He proceeds to follow the instructions. A wide smile paints his face as he looks up at the GoPal coordinator with a sense of achievement after applying the mixture. "The plant will be big in a few weeks," he says, beaming with joy.

* * *

It is midday, the sun shining hotter than ever at the Tenkasi district of TamilNadu. Tenkasi has not seen much rain this monsoon. "How has the production been?" inquires a GoPals coordinator. Periaswamy, a smallholder farmer, wipes a few beads of sweat with the handkerchief he has drawn from his pocket. "It has been great," he responds. "Thanks to your organization we were able to lease land for small scale production of Panchgavya products," he adds.

Periaswamy gestures to the coordinator to walk along with him. They both walk over to a small shed housing about 20 cows of the Kangeyam breed. The coordinator looks at the cows as Periaswamy continues, "I have been able to produce and sell so many types of eco products like lamps, dhoop sticks that are made from cow's by-products."

Periaswamy walks over to one of the cows. "Lamps have been a bestseller this month because of the upcoming Diwali season," he continues as he strokes the cow.

"They stopped producing milk over a year ago. I was ready to sell them to a butcher," he continues. He turns to face the cows as he battles tears of gratitude bubbling up from the pit of his stomach, making their way up the heart and throat to his eyes. "They are all my mothers, they continue to take good care of me." Periaswamy clears his throat. "The least I can do is love and care for them," he adds as he attempts to wipe a few tear drops from his eyes. The coordinator smiles, walks over to the cow and strokes her as he thinks, "This is one more step towards GoPals goals for saving cows of Indian origin and empowering farmers to build sustainable ecosystems."

CHAPTER TWELVE

PROTECTING CATTLE FROM BEING SLAUGHTERED IS A FUNDAMENTAL DUTY OF HUMANS

"Are you sure?" inquires Sai.

"Yes, the cattle market is going to involve much more native breeds this time. You better come prepared," says Ravi.

Sai puts his phone down. He stares outside the window at high-rise buildings in the far distance, painted in a golden hue as the sun prepares to set. A gentle breeze blows, bringing much solace to a hot, humid day. He corrects his hair and continues to stare into the sky as his thoughts drift. Scenes from his prior experience at the Melmalayanur cattle market flash before his eyes. He is reminded of his helplessness from that day as he stood surrounded by a loud crowd negotiating and selling cattle. He sees herds of cattle boarding a truck to be shipped away to Kerala, only to be slaughtered. He places a hand on his stomach as he struggles to avoid reminding himself about this incident. Tears roll down his eyes and his heart races as he battles the vision of a cow walking in the cattle market with blood soaked placenta after having given birth to a calf at the market.

He grips onto the window frame for support and takes a deep breath. Moments pass as he tries to console himself with the thought the mother and her calf were indeed saved that day. He closes his eyes, but sees the eyes of every cow and bull he had looked into that day as they were boarded into trucks to be crammed in a small space. He takes a deep breath, straightens himself, and wipes away the tears. "We have the capacity to be more prepared this time. I should get a team of people for errands and arrange for a lot of money this time around. We have to save as many cows as possible," he thinks to himself.

* * *

"You will be at the rescued cows' area. Keep tab on all the rescued cows," says Sai, to which Karthik and Vignesh respond with a nod.

"Ravi and I will navigate through the market and buy the cows. We will give a token to the buyer. That's your cue, Vishwa," Sai says, turning to his friend, Vishwanathan. "You will be in the car distributing cash to the people who give you the token," adds Sai.

The plan has been set. The team is ready as the market opens pre-dawn that rainy morning. Sai looks up at the dark sky with a heavy downpour drenching his rain jacket and takes a deep breath as he stands beside Ravi at the entrance to the market. They scan the market and see a clear separation in the type of cattle being sold or purchased. While one side had milching cows with their calves, the other was much larger in size and consisted of old, unyielding or sick cattle.

Sai wipes beads of sweat from his forehead and looks over at Ravi. They both nod and silently proceed to the larger section. Concealed in their silence are racing thoughts of apprehension filled with determination. They begin purchasing and within an hour manage to purchase over 50 cows. The news about Sai and Ravi buying cows spreads like fire, attracting more sellers towards them.

"I heard you are buying cows, want to look at mine?" asks one of the brokers, to which Sai responds, "Yes, they will go to the temple. How much?"

* * *

The sun begins to peek out as the rain continues to pour, making it slightly easier for Sai's team to function effectively. Sai and Ravi had already bought over 100 cows. "The clock is ticking," Sai thinks to himself as he continues to scan the market. He sees old and sick cattle being boarded into trucks from all sides. As he looks around, a truck with a lot of cows catches his attention. He nudges Ravi and they both run over to speak with a man making pointed gestures towards the cows as he spoke to another man who seemed like a truck driver.

"That is a lot of cows there, how many do you have," Sai strikes up a conversation. "This guy must be the dealer and the one he is talking with is maybe the truck driver," Sai thinks to himself as he continues to look for a response. "37," responds the man.

Sai brushes away the apathy in the response and continues to probe, "How much?" to which the man responds bluntly, "Not giving. Already sold to someone in Kerala." The response throws Sai back. "What do I do?" he staggers. "I need to think fast. There should be something that will convince this guy," he thinks to himself. Sai and Ravi plead and negotiate with the dealer. The dealer finally gives in to Sai's offer.

"Success!" Sai thinks to himself as he and Ravi walk away from the truck, continuing to scan the market. The final agreement came down to transporting the cattle to a cow shelter in Coimbatore instead of a butcher shop in Kerala. "It is almost dawn," says Ravi as he rubs away extra water from his drenched rain jacket. "Should we go over to the milching section?"

* * *

"We want all eight," says Sai. Ravi tears out a token to hand over to a butcher who had just purchased eight small calves, all of whom seemed like they were still feeding from their mothers but were separated for slaughter. The butcher smiles for having made much more profit in selling the calves to Sai and Ravi.

The cattle market finally closes at 10 AM. Sai and his friends look at all the 161 cows they had managed to save that morning. A radiant smile crosses their faces as they look at each other, but is shortly put out with the thoughts of transporting the saved cattle to nearby cow shelters.

They meticulously triage and load the drenched and hungry cows into about eight trucks and strategize the quickest way to get the cattle home.

* * *

Days pass. Sai has just returned from yet another rescue operation. He walks over to his home temple and stares into his spiritual master's photo as he reflects on a tough conversation he had had with the owner of one of the cow shelters earlier that day. "Depending on cow shelters for housing rescued cattle is not a sustainable solution," he thinks to himself. "His Holiness, I request you to please guide me as I navigate this path," he continues to reflect. He closes his eyes and sits in silence as he calms several thoughts racing through his mind. Moments pass as he drifts into calmness.

He finally breaks out of the stillness and opens his eyes to look at his spiritual master's photo. A thought crosses his mind as he continues to stare into the photo frame. "Perhaps, we could work with organic farmers, the poor and needy. Maybe they would be able to house the cattle, but I would have to advocate for how they can do that without much overload in terms of expenses," he contemplates. "Cow shelters are only going to find it difficult to incur added costs for every rescued cattle we bring into their facility. Cows and bulls are great partners for farmers. I should advocate for farmers to use cow waste to support organic farming. Besides, bulls can be used to support ploughing," he muses.

"There are so many families that cannot afford to buy cattle for their farming needs. This will be a great opportunity," he mulls over the idea. "But how am I going to get trustworthy people to implement these ideas? I wouldn't be surprised if a farmer in need of money ends up selling a rescued bull!" he thinks to himself. He gets excited and calls his friend Vishwanathan to continue brainstorming the idea.

* * *

"They are great, they help me prepare the land," Kapali says as he looks over at two rescued bulls stationed at the back of his house. Sai is visiting Kapali's farm. He had engaged a team of volunteers to build a network of vetted farmers who are positioned to house rescued cattle. Sai looks through a stack of papers with leasing agreements documenting the names, locations, cattle types, and duration for housing the rescued cattle. He finds Kapali's paperwork and brings it to the top of the stack so he has the formal agreement for reference.

Sai looks over at the farm neighboring Kapali's house and says, "Seems like you have ploughed recently," to which Kapila nods with approval. Sai walks over to the bulls and places one of his hands on a bull as he looks into the bull's eyes. Contrary to bulls being aggressive by nature, the two bulls at Kapali's house are calm. They don't move, but they respond to Sai's presence with respect. The serenity offered by the bull's eyes automatically brings tears to Sai's eyes as it does to the bull.

They exchange tears of gratitude as Sai thinks to himself, "Cows and bulls are indeed docile, compassionate beings. This 4-year journey of executing my duty as a human being in serving and rescuing cattle has been the most gratifying experience. This wouldn't have been possible without His Holiness's blessings. I only wish to continue this duty and engage more people to participate in protecting the cattle."

ABOUT THE AUTHOR

The author is a user experience researcher at an American multinational technology company. She holds a PhD in Human-Computer Interaction from Indiana University and a Masters in Computer Science from Miami University. For over a decade she has worked in multiple domains, focusing her work on uncovering people's behaviors, needs, and motivations to build intuitive and enjoyable products and services that empower people and change their lives in meaningful ways.

Two years ago, she accidentally landed on an online spiritual discourse by a well-renowned Vedic Scholar, which planted the seed for her to embark on a lifelong quest in advocating for human-cow friendship through acts of love and selfless service. She continues to volunteer in-person and remotely assists in different capacities, multiple cow shelters and sanctuaries across the globe. This book is her first endeavor at advocating for reviving the broken relationship between humans, cows and bulls.

For more information visit
https://www.befriendcows.com/

Made in the USA
Las Vegas, NV
18 April 2023

70754031R00049